Russian In

Русский язык в моей жизни

David Talks

DEDICATION

To my fellow interpreters in the RNR.

RUSSIAN IN MY LIFE

CONTENTS

RUSSIAN IN MY LIFE

RUSSIAN IN MY LIFE

PREFACE

"Probably a spy".

I have heard this said, even within my own family! So it's about time I tried to set the record straight. Russian has undoubtedly been an important feature of my life, but where did it all begin?

1. MARCHING ORDERS

National Service was compulsory for young men between 1951 and 1960. Fortunately I found out about the Russian Language course in the services from a friend who thoroughly recommended it. It seemed (and turned out to be) a very positive way of spending two years before taking up a place at Worcester College, Oxford, to read Modern Languages.

I registered for National Service in the Navy. Over a nine year period more than 1,500 Navy men followed one or other of the interpreter/translator routes. A good number of them were drafted after leaving sixth form in which they had studied French and often one other language. I had taken 'A' levels in French and German at Mercers School in London.

However, before the Russian courses could start, there was much to be done. There was, of course, a medical examination. This involved a brisk and efficient poke about one's person, and was followed by an interview and an IQ test. The test included prose to be précis-ed, numbers to be manipulated and shapes to be reassembled.

Quite soon I was called up to the Vicky Barracks (the Victoria Royal Naval Barracks in Portsmouth) for three weeks' basic training.

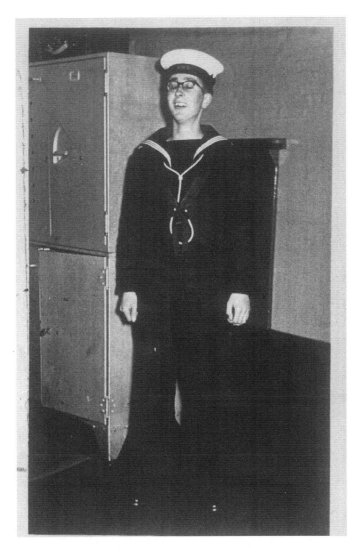

Author, Victoria RNB, Portsmouth, November 1956

I received a Navy number, pay book (which served also as an official identity document, but without a photo) and uniform. This consisted of bell-bottom trousers, a traditional peak-less sailor's cap with HMS Victory on the cap-band, plus a raincoat (a Burberry), socks and boots. We were also given a working uniform, so-called no. 8s, comprising navy blue cotton trousers and a much lighter blue, heavy-duty cotton shirt with buttoned pockets. To sew on badges or for any running repairs we were provided with a 'hussif' (housewife), containing thread, needles and buttons. There were also brushes and tins of boot polish. To carry all this gear we had a large kitbag.

In those three weeks at Portsmouth we received inoculations – I remember a queue of sailors lining up for these and one sailor failing to move on and so receiving several jabs – he finally fainted! We came to realise that the people actually in charge were the petty officers and chief petty officers (the equivalent of sergeants in the Army) - thank goodness they were friendly. In the evenings some of us listened to recitals of classical music on records organised by the padre. A highlight was a visit to HMS Victory.

We also learnt to drill to a bewildering array of parade ground commands. Marching looks an easy enough skill, but in every batch of coder specials (that is what we were called) there were always one or two who were unable to coordinate the movement of arms and legs. The effort to get it right would lead some wretch to lead with his left arm and left leg at the same time: the resulting chaos would render the drill instructor apoplectic. There were those who looked like a sack of potatoes, failed to slope arms properly ("by yer left udder, you clown, not that udder, de udder

udder"), or even dropped their rifle ("you are the only one of its kind in captivity") or failed to co-ordinate arms and legs ("The Russians had this trouble. Forget 'Left, Right'. They tied hay on one arm and straw on the other and shouted 'Hay, Straw'...."). Basic training did have its humorous moments.[1]

The end of our basic training found us ready for the Russian course at the Joint Services School for Languages at Crail in Fife, Scotland. However, JSSL was not quite ready for us, so as probationary coders we had to fill in time. We went to HMS Mercury, a signals station and school near East Meon in Hampshire. We did not have time for the cryptography course, so I spent a week feeding pigs, sweeping leaves in a wood (in a November gale!) and playing table tennis.

---

[1] Adapted from 'The Coder Special Archive' p.40

2. TO SCOTLAND

Finally I travelled by steam train to Crail. The JSSL was housed in a converted Fleet Air Arm station, perched on the rocky coast and run by the Army. Our new intake (about fifty of us from all three services) was greeted by the Army Commandant with these words: "Welcome to JSSL, Crail. Now, if you play ball with me, I'll play ball with you, but remember – it's my ball!" Our naval contingent was now under the command of Commander Maitland-Makgill-Crichton DSO, DSC – an impressive man who spoke twelve languages, while our round white caps now bore the name of HMS Cochrane, our depot 'ship' for pay and admin, based in Rosyth.

On one occasion a small group of us were sentenced to three days' potato peeling for being late on parade. At 11 o'clock on the final evening we joined in a potato fight in the nissen hut where we were housed and then realised that we would have to clear up the mess before the morning inspection. On another occasion, I remember with shame that we carried a drunken coder out of the hut, took his bed to pieces, reassembled it in the middle of a nearby ploughed field, so that he woke up next morning with no idea how he had got to such a place. Eighteen-year-olds will be boys!

Commander Maitland-Makgill-Crichton DSO, DSC and Mr Diakovsky. 1957

But our primary concern was to learn the Russian language. My first experience of this came when a Polish exile, Henryk A. Malhomme (de la Roche), who had joined the Polish free forces in Britain and was four times decorated for bravery, put us through our paces. He went from desk to desk asking each student: "У вас есть карандаш?" Nobody could answer, until he came to Nicholas Pasternak Slater, who, in perfect Russian, said that yes, he had a pencil!

Of the fifteen Polish teachers on the 1956 Crail list, the most memorable was the flamboyant ex-colonel Josef Godlewski, who gave us the impression that he had once, almost single-handedly, prevented the Russians from capturing Warsaw.

In all there were fifty-three men and four women on the staff. Nearly half were said to be Russian, of whom thirteen were specifically designated 'ex-Soviet' and one stateless. Eight were from the Baltic States – Estonia, Latvia and Lithuania – and two from the Ukraine. Eight were British and there was a solitary Czech. During language training a coder would have direct dealings with only four or five tutors for grammar, conversation and dictation practice. There were also general lectures, singing sessions, (often led by Mr. Diakovsky) and other extra-curricular activities, such as the Russian choir and drama productions. I still remember with pleasure a handful of Russian folksongs, their words and exciting melodies and rhythms.

Our teachers, who had experienced revolutions, civil wars, imprisonment and torture, could hardly fail to impress young men whose furthest journey from home had, in many cases, been to report to naval barracks in Portsmouth. We listened to their life stories and were impressed. A certain Mr. Ross (not his real name) revealed that he had been forced by the Germans to fight against his own people, the Russians. He decided to escape and ended in a hospital where the slightly wounded lay on one side of the ward and the seriously wounded lay on the other. He knew that the slightly wounded would eventually be sent back to the front. So, to avoid this, he poured boiling oil over his leg in order to be classed with the seriously wounded. After many further adventures he ended up in JSSL Crail.

Another impressive teacher was Prince Valentin Volkonsky who had served in the Czarist navy during World War I. He chewed tobacco in class and spat into empty Gold Block tins on the desks. He looked like an eighteenth century grandee, with a hooked nose, scraped-back hair and exquisite manners (apart from the spitting!) A gold watch and a gold-headed cane were all that remained of the Volkonsky inheritance.

The majority of us achieved proficiency in Russian – testament to the teaching methods and materials used. Mastering the Russian alphabet was no problem. Of the thirty three letters, largely derived from Greek, six are effectively the same as in English. Another six temptingly look the same, but are pronounced differently e.g. 'c' sounds like 's' in 'swim', 'h' like 'n', 'y' like 'oo'. The remaining twenty one are novel, the most outlandish being Ж, usually represented in English as 'zh', the sound made by 's' in 'pleasure'. We quickly realised that quite a few Russian words have roots in common with English – 'mat' for mother, 'brat' for brother, 'syestra' for sister, 'dom' for house. Those of us who knew Latin or German could readily appreciate that Russian grammar was similar; we saw that nouns and adjectives change their endings depending on their role in a sentence, whether, for example, they are subjects, objects, possessives or follow prepositions. There was a lot more to learn about verbs in particular, but for six hours a day we persevered, taking progress tests every two weeks.

The school badge

Lesson in progress 1957. Left to right, Angus McEwen, Dick Haddon, John Symonds, Prince Volkonsky.

We all had a powerful incentive not to be kicked out of the JSSL. Failure in tests could result in a 'return to unit'. This could be an unfortunate fate for a soldier in the 1950s when there was fighting in Korea, Malaya, Cyprus, with the Mau

Mau in Kenya etc. The fate of a failed coder was not so difficult to contemplate: being forced to tend the diesel engine of a warship as a stoker was the frequently quoted threat. I managed to survive the tests and stayed in Crail, while some of my colleagues left to train as translators and eavesdroppers by the Kiel Canal or in Cuxhaven.

Crail 1957, before the translators left.
Alan Woodrow, John Slater, ?, David Fairhall, ?.
?, ?, John Young, John Symonds, the author, Brian Taylor, John Graham,
Angus McEwen
Dick Haddon, Macauley, Chris Willoughby

But there was more to life than Russian. There was the rum ration, known as 'grog'. The entitlement was a daily 'tot' (one eighth of a pint) of dark Caribbean rum diluted with a quarter of a pint of water. This custom was only abolished in 1970, modern machinery being incompatible with groggy sailors!

Ray Adams, Chris Willoughby, Diakovsky, Dick Haddon, Commander M-M-C, John Kendall, Jack McWhor, Prince Volkonsky, Jack Evans, Ian Philips, Will Morris
Keith Grant, Frank Knowles, the author, Macauley, John Symons, Henry Greenfield, Angus McEwen

There were also day visits to ships in Rosyth. I remember a day on an inshore minesweeper, sweeping mines in the Firth of Forth in a force 8 gale. I asked a sailor how to avoid sea-sickness: he said, "Keep your eye on the horizon and chew breadcrumbs". These visits were designed to give us first-hand experience of the Navy, (equipment, tactics, etc.), so that we could match up our knowledge of naval Russian with reality.

At some stage in 1957 we were promoted to leading coders (special), with a consequent hike in pay. The pay enabled us to enjoy something of the pleasures of life in Crail, and especially in St. Andrew's, which was about ten miles away. In St. Andrew's we tried a little golf, ate pie and chips in a café (for 1/6d old money), and eventually met some of the students at the university.

The author missing a hole in 2, St Andrews 1957

There now occurred a life-changing event in my life, for I met my wife Audrey at a university 'hop' (dance). She was studying for a degree in history. The relationship prospered and we spent much time (when I could get away from Crail) in each other's company, walking, talking, bird-watching, eating hot doughnuts direct from the bakery, enjoying

Audrey's cooking (maybe roast wood pigeon), and inevitably I sometimes missed the last bus back to Crail. This meant a ten-mile walk at night and not too much sleep before the 7a.m. parade next morning. Watching the sun rise over the North Sea and the coast of Fife served as some sort of compensation.

The final Civil Service Commission exams came and went. I did fairly well in the exam but not well enough to be called an Interpreter First Class. Nevertheless, in August 1958 I was commissioned as a Midshipman RNVR (soon to become RNR). I remember very little of the interview for this, except the question, "If you were leading a group of walkers in the mountains, would you do it from behind or in front?"

What to do with us now? Quite a few of us went on courses to learn interrogation techniques. The Intelligence Corps' base at Maresfield, Sussex boasted a newly-established 'Intelligence Research Unit'. The Admiralty chose this Army camp to instill into National Service midshipmen the skills necessary to prise information out of captives taken in war. The course consisted largely of lectures, films and demonstrations. The Geneva Convention on the treatment of prisoners was frequently quoted. The course included a three-day exercise. Our group of naval interpreters was divided into two. I was on the 'British side' and the other half (which consisted, of course, of our friends and fellow-linguists) was deemed to be on the 'Russian side'. As part of the 'softening-up' process, at one point (I am ashamed to say), we put our 'prisoners' into horizontal lockers and ran up and down on the lockers. The 'British side' was tasked with extracting certain information from the 'Russian side' – all in Russian, of course. I remember interrogating a friend,

Frank Knowles (later Professor of Linguistics and future Vice-Chancellor of Aston University). He became so exasperated by this process that he upset the desk where we sat and ran out of the building (where in real circumstances he would have been shot by a sentry).

As an ironic footnote to this experience, in 2010 I met the car park attendant at Norwich School (in the Cathedral Close) who turned out to be Russian. He told me, in Russian, that he had been a tank commander and engineer in the Soviet army and that he had come to England after the break-up of the Soviet Union, when morale in the army was low and pay was in arrears. He said that he had been trained as an interrogator of possible British prisoners-of-war and I replied that I had been trained as an interrogator of possible Russian prisoners-of-war. We had a good laugh about this and were glad that the Cold War had remained cold.

3. TO THE ADMIRALTY

There were still a few months of National Service left. I was posted to the Admiralty in London and signed the Official Secrets Act. My work consisted of helping to plot movements of Soviet shipping (merchant ships and warships) all over the world on a large wall map, guided by reports received from GCHQ Cheltenham, and probably eavesdroppers in Cuxhaven. At that time the Soviet navy was regularly probing our defences and while Audrey was on holiday with her family in Alnwick, they heard that a Russian trawler had come aground on the Northumberland coast. They went to look at the trawler, I saw it on the Admiralty plot, and we all wondered what that Soviet fishing vessel was fishing for!

We operated in the bowels of the Admiralty, under the Citadel in the Mall. I walked to work in civvies from a Navy-rented flat in Chelsea, arriving at 10 a.m. for coffee with some American liaison officers. On one occasion there was what was called a 'flap' in the Yemen. This would have been the state of emergency declared in May 1958 by the Governor of Aden, then a British colony, which had been attacked by Yemeni tribesmen. Consequently I was asked to spend a few nights in the Citadel rabbit warren. One night, at about 2 a.m., the phone rang. Hesitatingly I answered. A voice from afar said, "There is an unidentified submarine approaching the north-east coast of England. What should I do about it?" As a very green nineteen-year-old I had no idea, so I replied, "What would you do?" "Send out a Shackleton, Sir," came the response. (The Shackleton was the reconnaissance aircraft of the period.) "Good idea," I said and that was the end of the phone call. To this day I have no idea what happened; my report the following day was met with apparent indifference.

The Admiralty Citadel, London

While at the Admiralty I nearly bumped into Earl Mountbatten. I was leaving the Admiralty by a back entrance into the Mall. I was dressed in civvies, wearing my by now somewhat battered Burberry and carrying two suitcases. A car swept to a halt and out stepped Mountbatten in full uniform, 'scrambled egg' up to his elbows. I then did a foolish thing – I dropped my suitcases and saluted. You should not salute when wearing civvies. The Earl looked stern, but said nothing.

4. OXFORD AND THE RNR

I had been offered a place to read French and German at Worcester College, Oxford, but after two years of study and practice of Russian felt I could never know another language as well as I knew Russian, so switched to read French and Russian. At the same time I joined the Royal Naval Reserves (RNR) as a Russian interpreter. In November 1959 I was made a Sub-Lieutenant RNR and in November a Lieutenant RNR. My reservist courses began, firstly at Crail, then at RAF Tangmere, then at Beaconsfield (the Defence School of Languages), then at the Britannia Royal Naval College in Dartmouth.

Every year we were put through our Russian paces and examined. I am glad to say that by 1967 I had achieved first class standard, and was described in the post-course reports as "industrious, friendly, loyal, keen, with a considerably improved knowledge of Russian naval terminology." I enjoyed these two week refresher courses very much. I remember, one afternoon during a Beaconsfield course, sitting in the Saville Garden in Windsor (this was a Wednesday afternoon – devoted to sport, etc.) thinking to myself, while taking tea, that I was being paid twice for my conscientious studies!

Beaconsfield 1966
?, Dick Haddon, Mark Evans, the author, Royle, Philby, ?, Brain Baxendale
Ron Truman, Geoff Wickham, Tony Bosworth, Creasey, Adrian Room,
Geoff Forbes, Ray Adams

The courses at Dartmouth were highlights. Friendships were renewed, pink gins drunk, Russian course material mastered. I was even commissioned to paint a watercolour of the view from the College of the Dart estuary to hang in the wardroom!

Britannia Royal Naval College, Dartmouth

On one occasion a carload of uniformed officers drove from Dartmouth to an 'acquaint' course in Portsmouth (a course to familiarise ourselves with warships). We stopped at the entrance to the Royal Naval dockyard and were asked to provide an I.D. None of us had anything to prove we were legitimate visitors. Then, in a pocket, I found my Worcester College Oxford Punt Club membership card. This was enough: we were allowed in!

I recall one Easter course which took place shortly before the passing out parade of Dartmouth officers under training. A notice went up to announce the visit to the College on the Saturday of the Emir of Al Bahan. Nobody had heard of the place but we accepted it, as the College trained many future naval officers from the Emirates. Then a further notice was pinned up, postponing the visit to the Sunday and strengthening the security state of the College. On Sunday, during the Anglican service in the College chapel, I witnessed the entry of the Emir, accompanied by minders fingering revolvers in their flowing robes and also by the Captain of the College, Captain Julian Oswald (later to become First Sea Lord). I thought it curious that an Emir should attend an Anglican service. During coffee on the 'quarter deck', the Emir made a speech through an interpreter. All the officers and staff were present. The Emir spoke of his pleasure in visiting the College, but, he said, he was horrified by the dreadful conditions under which the officers-in-training had to work. Jaws dropped. Breath was held. In view of this, said the Emir, he would like to present to the College a cheque for one.......... penny! Only then did people realise that this was a hoax. It was an April Fools Day joke, set up by the Captain of the College himself, as a morale booster before the passing out parade. I spoke to the 'Emir' later. He was a lieutenant from the Ark Royal!

In 1969 I was promoted to Lieutenant-Commander. In 1973 I was awarded the Reserve Decoration. I wear the medal with pride on Remembrance Sunday in Norwich Cathedral. In 1985 I was awarded a Clasp to the Reserve Decoration.

Spring 1976, Dartmouth
Tony Bosworth, ?, Chris Clarke, Steve Penny
John Hicks, Tony Taylor, Alex Rutherford, David Wanstall, the author

I wish I could still get into the uniform!

B.R.N.C RNR Russian course, Easter 1978

Dartmouth 1979
The author, Tony Charlier, Roland Beckingham, John Hicks
Petr Kostantinoff, Alex Rutherford, Robert Avery

Dartmouth July 1981: Ron Truman, Roland Beckingham, Chris Clarke, Tony
Bosworth, Bryan Baxendale, Peter Hill
Robert Avery, the author, Anthony Charlier, Tony Holcombe, Paul Jenkins
Alex Rutherford, Count Nikolai Sologub, Geoff Windsor, David Wanstall

HMS Dryad, July 1982: Tony Bosworth, Mike Eager, Chris Clarke
Nigel Hawkins, Brian Baxendale, John Mott, Peter Hill
Mike Carter, the author, Tony Holcombe, Roland Beckingham, Robert
Avery

The reservist Russian interpreters were stood down in 1985, as part of the 'peace dividend', when Russia was no longer seen as a serious threat. At the end of the last course in Dartmouth, we had a special dinner at the Carved Angel in which the FRINTON Society was born. (FRINTON stands for Former Russian Interpreters Of the Navy). The Frinton Society has since met for dinners in many parts of Britain and even at Faslane on a nuclear submarine, HMS Sceptre.

Frinton Society on HMS Sceptre

Here we posed for a group photograph on the upper casing before going down two long and steep ladders to the wardroom, where we were given a horse's neck (brandy and ginger ale), the traditional drink of submariners. On a submarine there is no dining room, so we ate our meal in the operations room, propped against banks of switches. We were then taken on a guided tour and introduced to the idea of 'hot bunking', where each bunk was occupied by a man for eight hours, so three men in twenty-four hours and beneath each bunk three lockers for their possessions. The question was asked: "What makes a good submariner?" The reply came: "It helps to be small." Then we went on to view the missiles and the reactor. HMS Sceptre was at that time in Faslane but would later be leaving for the Caribbean.

I very much enjoyed my time in the RNR. We were a sort of insurance policy in case the Cold War should turn hot. We were even sent instructions as to where we should report in the event of an emergency.

5. TEACHING RUSSIAN

At the same time as serving in the RNR, I was teaching French and Russian at Gresham's School at Holt in Norfolk and then at Rugby School. There I had small numbers of students of Russian preparing for A Levels and university entrance. While at Rugby, in 1974, I went to Moscow with a group of staff and pupils.

The Moscow River, Moscow.

As everything seemed to close in the evenings, we went out to see if there was any entertainment available. From a bridge over the Moscow River I saw a vessel advertising 'Gipsy ensemble': this seemed promising. We went on board, past a soldier with a sub-machine gun, and came to a space which was in almost total darkness. At one end a gipsy band was playing. Numerous drunken Russians lay with their heads on round tables. We found an alcove with a table and chairs and I ordered a bottle of Soviet champagne. As we opened this, the cork exploded and hit a fluorescent light fitting, which crashed down on to the table, smashing the glasses. Not only that, but the light came on. This was in the depths of the Cold War. There was a moment of shock, and then we all burst into laughter, thanks to the incongruity of our situation. What do you think happened next? Nothing. The gipsy band continued to play and none of the drunken Russians moved. I apologised to a waitress who eventually emerged, but she said not to worry, that such things often happened there. We crept back to our hotel to learn that we should not have been in such a place!

Occasionally English schools received visits from Russian students and teachers. I remember particularly a visit from Voronezh in Russia, which is known as a 'hero city' in the same way as Coventry, because it suffered so greatly in World War II. Groups from Voronezh were visiting Eton, Rugby and Manchester Grammar School. I planned a week of lessons in which the Russians could participate along with our pupils. To our surprise, we received a visit from a coach load of Russians who were by no means of school age and who were not studying English. They were shepherded by a 'minder', who was obviously a member of the KGB, and there was only one member of the group who spoke adequate English, so he could act as an interpreter. It seems that the group were good party members, who were being rewarded for their loyalty by this 'holiday' in Britain. So I had to scrap the prepared timetable and replace it with a series of excursions together with a few 'lessons'. However, they seemed mostly happy to spend their time window-shopping in Rugby's 'picturesque' high street, where they spent their money on trainers and portable radios. They also ate in the boarding houses and were entertained by the Headmaster, whose opulent house amazed them. Every evening ended with the singing of Russian songs. When it was time to leave there were tears. The contrast between their normal life and this glimpse of western life was clearly an emotional experience.

6. TO NORWICH

Since 1988, when we moved to Norwich, there have been fewer opportunities to speak Russian, though at one time the Cathedral had links with churches in Tbilisi in Georgia and groups from Tbilisi would come to visit. Although the Georgian language is very different from Russian, all Georgians had been exposed to Russian and some were more comfortable speaking in Russian than in English. We used to like taking these Georgian visitors to Walsingham, where there are three Orthodox shrines. The earliest is in the Anglican shrine and was created for the Polish airmen who were based in North Norfolk during World War II, the second is in the former railway station and the third is in a former Methodist chapel in Great Walsingham.

On one occasion we had a visit from the Chanters Group of the Church of St. Panteleimon the Healer in Tbilisi. We took them to Walsingham and they sang in each of the shrines and concluded by singing in the refectory in the Anglican Shrine to thank the chef for his cooking.

The Anglican Shrine, Walsingham

Chanters Group of the Church of St. Panteleimon the Healer in Tbilisi.

So Russian has continued to play a part in my life, even in Norwich. However there is now little opportunity for me to refresh my language skills. But I remain very grateful for my Russian experience. Not a spy, though; in fact, you could say, just the opposite!

AND AFTERWARDS

Norwich Cathedral by the author

In 1988 I began another career as a painter. I have been lucky enough to paint in France, Italy, North Africa and the Far East. I have exhibited with the Royal Institute of Painters in Watercolours London, with the Royal Society of Marine Artists London, and also at the Norwich Castle Museum. I am a Past President of the Rugby and District Art Society and a former Chairman and later President of the Norfolk and Norwich Art Circle. From 1998 to 2008, I held an annual one-man exhibition at the Galerie L'Espinasse in Rouen. I have arranged exhibitions for East Anglian artists in Rouen and for Rouen artists in Norwich, as part of the Norwich-Rouen twinning link. I exhibit regularly with the Norfolk and Norwich Art Circle, at the Norfolk Show and with the East Anglian Group of Marine Artists. I have a website: www.davidtalks.co.uk

ACKNOWLEDGEMENTS

I am grateful to my wife, Audrey, who has put these memories on her computer, to my grandson, Alphaeus, who has prepared the map and to my son, Martin, who has produced this book

I am grateful for the help I received from 'The Coder Special Archive', Cash and Gerrard, Hodgson Press, 2012.

Produced by My Saga

Tell your saga.

Printed in Poland
by Amazon Fulfillment
Poland Sp. z o.o., Wrocław